Komiete Tetteh

The Usefulness of Market Failure in Explaining Government Action

A Critical Evaluation

GRIN Verlag

Bibliografische Information der Deutschen Nationalbibliothek:

Die Deutsche Bibliothek verzeichnet diese Publikation in der Deutschen National-
bibliografie; detaillierte bibliografische Daten sind im Internet über http://dnb.d-
nb.de/ abrufbar.

Imprint:

Copyright © 2013 GRIN Verlag GmbH
Druck und Bindung: Books on Demand GmbH, Norderstedt Germany
ISBN: 978-3-656-53576-8

This book at GRIN:

http://www.grin.com/en/e-book/263574/the-usefulness-of-market-failure-in-
explaining-government-action

GRIN - Your knowledge has value

Der GRIN Verlag publiziert seit 1998 wissenschaftliche Arbeiten von Studenten, Hochschullehrern und anderen Akademikern als eBook und gedrucktes Buch. Die Verlagswebsite www.grin.com ist die ideale Plattform zur Veröffentlichung von Hausarbeiten, Abschlussarbeiten, wissenschaftlichen Aufsätzen, Dissertationen und Fachbüchern.

Visit us on the internet:

http://www.grin.com/

http://www.facebook.com/grincom

http://www.twitter.com/grin_com

The Usefulness of Market Failure in Explaining Government Action: A Critical Evaluation

By

Komiete Tetteh

Abstract

This paper contributes to the discourse on the usefulness of market failure as an explanatory and justificatory tool for public policy and government action. Critically examining and evaluating market failure's theoretical robustness, ideological underpinnings, institutional claims and practical application, it argues that while the tool offers some insights into what governments (can) do, it fails to provide a compelling answer to the fundamental question of why governments exist. It is suggested that alternative approaches and theorizations such as institutional political economy approach, historical inquiry and empirical studies of the state offer more comprehensive explanations for understanding the role and relationship between the state and the market.

Key words: market failure, state invention, neoliberalism, efficiency

1. Preamble

Market failure—the notion that markets fail to allocate resources efficiently to meet societal ideals—is a mainstream logic for interpreting and justifying state action. This reasoning, plus the need to ensure equity, has been described by the World Bank as 'the economic rationale for state intervention' (World Bank, 1997 p. 26), and is frequently used by governments, politicians and influential international organizations, including the World Bank and the International Monetary Fund (IMF), in their various policy prescriptions for tackling myriad socio-economic maladies. Market failure is also often cited in the wider debate over what the appropriate size, role and scope or powers of government should be, with each position being constructed on the basis of some form of market failure. However, others flaw the entire argument as presenting a narrow neo-liberalistic view of the market, based on some shaky assumptions, intended to defend and perpetuate the injustices of the market system and therefore advocate alternative theorizations for explaining government action.

1

This paper makes a contribution to the discourse on the effectiveness of market failure as an explanatory and justificatory tool for state action. In doing so, section 2 examines and analyzes market failure's central doctrine, including its underlying ideas about the structure and behavior of the 'normative market', as well as its purported shortcomings from which the role and scope of government is derived. This is followed by Section 3, which considers the different ways in which market failure is applied in the design of public policy. A critique of market failure is offered in section 4, drawing mainly on existing arguments for and against market failure in the literature. In section 5, I present my judgment on the usefulness of market failure in explaining state action, employing four evaluation criteria: the reasonability of its assumptions; effectiveness in explaining the origins of the state; internal coherency; and applicability. I argue on the basis of what the theory says or is in relation to each of these criteria, that although market failure is a useful tool that provides some insight on what kind of activities can be undertaken by the state, the theory makes unrealistic (and flawed) assumptions about the market, the state and motivations driving public action; is laden with internal contradictions; and suffers from ambiguity regarding the acceptable point of state intervention, thereby rendering it an inadequate public policy manual, even where its capitalist ideology is imbibed. I then propose the use of alternative theorizations, including both inductive and deductive theories, in better explaining public policy and government action (section 6), and offer my concluding comments in section 7.

2. Overview of Market Failure Theory

To understand what market failure is, it is useful first to consider what the mainstream economic model of the market is. The ideal market, in mainstream or neoclassical economic thought, is— or supposed to be—a voluntary and self-regulated exchange system whose defining structure, and ultimate test of efficiency, is perfect competition. Perfect competitive markets are characterized by many buyers and sellers with none having any market power; perfect information; and the determination of prices through free bargain[1]. Because free competitive markets, through the interplay of the forces of demand and supply, set the price of goods and services and output levels at an equilibrium point where both producer profit and consumer

---

[1] The other structural characteristics of a perfect competitive market include: product homogeneity; ease of entry and exist; freedom of choice; long-run factor mobility; zero transaction cost; well defined and transferable property rights; and self-interested, rational actors (i.e., firms and consumers) driven by the motive of profit and utility maximization respectively

welfare are maximized, market economists argue they are the most rewarding and efficient of all market types, efficiently and allocatively, in the long run. Productive efficiency is where firms are able to produce a good at the lowest average total cost possible. Allocative efficiency on the other hand is where the amount of goods produced in the market is commensurate with total societal demand, such that marginal consumer benefit equates marginal producer cost[2].

At the same time, however, because this is often not the case (since all the requirements necessary for perfect competition may, after all, not be present), and because *private* optimum level of production and consumption excludes but affects *social* optimality, market failure is always said to occur. From a public policy point of view, it is the inability of the markets to deliver *all* the goods and services desired by society, and or to provide them in ways that do not *negatively* impact society as a whole (Hughes, 2003).

Market failure, then, is a systemic deficiency of the market system, attributed to the internal structural organization and behavior of actors, which is ubiquitous and bound to persist (Foldvary, 2006) without any outside intervention. In principle, violation of any of the conditions or principles underlying perfect competition amount to market failure; however, four major types of market failure are recognized in the literature. They are:

Monopoly
The incidence of monopoly, the situation whereby a single firm or a small number of them (oligopoly) dominate the market for a particular good or service, is considered a form of market failure. Monopolies emerge when sellers are able to lower the unit cost of an additional good or service provided over a range of output, due to technological superiority or economies of scale from activities with large fixed costs and no viable substitute. Utility providers such as water and electricity suppliers and airline companies are respective examples of firms in monopolistic and oligopolistic markets. These can exploit their cost advantage and market power to engage in anti-consumer welfare and anti-competitive practices, such as reducing output to keep prices and profits high, product tying, lowering product quality, predatory pricing and collusion, if unchecked.

---

[2] This is also known as 'Pareto efficiency', named after the Italian economist Vilfredo Pareto who defined it as the condition whereby it is impossible to make some one better off without making another person at least worse off.

Public Goods

These are goods which, once produced, are simultaneously available to all members of society. They are non-excludable (meaning that non-payers can neither be effectively prevented from accessing it nor practically be charged based upon use) and non-rival (in the sense that consumption by one person does not reduce the total amount available to others). Street light and defence are examples of such. The problem of 'free riding' acts as a disincentive for market provision of public goods, leading to zero or under-supply of public goods. Thus, other mechanisms outside the free price system would have to be used to provide or pay for public goods. A similar argument is applied to the provision of merit goods such as education and health care and regulation of common property goods (e.g. fishery, forest) which the markets, if left to supply and manage, will fail to do so optimally[3].

Externalities

These are spill-over effects of market transactions on third parties or the environment (Hughes, 2003), which are not accounted for in the private costs and benefits of those activities. Secondary smoking and immunization are examples of negative and positive externality.

Imperfect information

Information or knowledge is key to the survival of the market system. But when information is unavailable, limited, wrong or misleading information, especially to consumers, it can lead to under-consumption of certain goods or cause harm. Or, when either the buyer or seller of a good or service has superior knowledge over the other and exploits the imbalance to their advantage. This is known as information asymmetry. Examples of this include a doctor prescribing more services than a patient actually needs, or an arts collector buying for next to nothing a masterpiece from a junk store that has no idea of its real value), which can cause inefficient

---

[3] Merit goods are excludable but non-rival, meaning that can be delivered by the private sector (e.g., private clinics). However, because the public benefit (or the multiplier effects) from individual consumption of merit goods exceeds private gains (for instance, the GDP contributions from having a highly skilled and healthy population exceeds the job and income benefits to the individual), which buyers base their decision on, this can lead to under-consumption and thus under-supply of merit goods. Moreover, leaving their provision in the hands of the market where *ability to pay*, rather than *need* determines how much and who gets to consume what is produced, pose equity problems, not considering the higher social cost of failing to educate the talented and insuring the highly skilled. Common property goods are non-excludable but rival; this implies that leaving them to the market will lead to their rapid depletion than if some collective arrangement is in place to regulate their use.

resource allocation. Other expressions of market failure resulting from asymmetric information are 'adverse selection'—where the buyer tends to exert 'abnormal' burden on a service provider (for example, sick people buying health insurance), and 'moral hazard'—a negative behavior that ensues once a safety mechanism is in place for the insured-against event (for example, reckless driving by insured car owners).

3. Public Policy Implications of Market Failure

The theory of market failure has been used to underwrite several government decisions, policies, programs and projects in different sectors and at different scales with the aim of addressing some sort of market failure. Five common types of policy interventions are:

Regulation

This is where the coercive powers of the state are used to compel, prohibit or control certain activities in the market (Hughes, 2003). Price control, pollution limits and smoking ban in some public facilities are examples of regulation. Apart from protecting consumer welfare and the environment, regulations can be used to level the playing field in a particular market or safeguard national (or even global) economic interest, as seen with the new US and European government banking laws, which are aimed at forestalling the reoccurrence of the recent global financial crisis and recession thought to be have been caused by reckless lending behavior of creditors.

Provision

Government can also provide certain non-market goods and services such as defence, education, physical infrastructure, law and order, and social security directly to its citizenry or a section of them.

Subsidy

Subsidies are used where government is unable, unwilling or ineffective in providing a good or service it desires and thus assists someone to do it (Hughes, 2003). They can also be used to stem the decline of certain industries (e.g., recent US government bailout of General Motors and Chrysler) or start new ones (e.g., grants to renewable energy companies). Like regulation, subsidies can come in different forms—cash benefits, tax breaks, research grants and low or interest-free loans.

Taxation

Imposing fees and charges on individuals and economic activities is another means of dealing with market failures, particularly externalities and public goods. Carbon tax, which is being implemented in many regions and countries, is one example that can be used to internalize the negative impact of CO_2 emissions from emitters. Similarly, property tax can be used to provide and maintain municipal services.

Other Applications of Market Failure

Apart from these expansionist polices that increase the level of government involvement in the private economy, market failure can also be used to scale back or shrink the size and government activities. Here, state activities which are 'thought' to belong to the private sector (typically production and some provision), are axed and or given to the private sector. This is a core component of the structural adjustment programs offered by the IMF and the World Bank particularly to debt-ridden developing nations, where austerity is combined with divestiture of state-owned enterprises.

Another way in which the theory of market failure is applied in public policy is introducing market principles to the modus-operandi and management of the public sector. Apart from contracting-out certain public sector functions to the private sector, efficiency, accountability and performance-based incentives become the new ethos of public management—part of the concept of new pubic management, which is market driven.

4. Critique of Market Failure

In critiquing market failure, it is first important to examine the various arguments and rationales that have been offered by supporters and opponents of the theory of market failure.

Supporting Views

A common argument used to support market failure theory derives from the fact that it provides a useful insight into understanding the workings of the market, including the behavior of its participants and the attributes of the various commodities and services produced and exchanged within it. The concept is also said to reveal the potency, efficiency and sustainability of the market system to allocate goods and services, even without government involvement. Moreover, by outlining a repertoire of corrective measures for rectifying market failures or lessening their impact on society, the theory offers useful pointers to what kind of activities the state can perform (Hughes, 2003).

Another practical justification that has been proffered to support market failure is that it helps to curb unnecessary government spending and control or state domination of the economy, which tends to be unproductive and inhibit innovation. Arguably, the increasing restructuring of government bureaucracy and the economies of former non-market states such as China in favour of the market principle, even if selective, is perhaps the greatest triumph of market failure argument.

Opposing Views

Criticisms of market failure are rife. However, for greater clarity, I have decided to put these into three major types or standpoints, namely: institutional/political, technical and practical viewpoints. Institutional and political criticisms challenge the underlying assumptions the theory makes about the market, the state and human motive. The centerpiece of the institutionalist argument advanced by institutional political economists such as Ha-Joon Chang and John Commons is that the market is an institution (rather than a system of rational individuals and firms in objective relations) shaped by a complex interaction of social, political, legal, economic and cultural institutions, values and norms, which together make up the economic system of which the market is just one component, and that the neoliberal attempt to decouple or alienate the market from its wider institutional and political context in which it is embedded results in treating as 'technicalities' problems that are 'political' in nature (see Chang, 2002; and Hughes, 2003).

Related to this is Chang's apt observation that the definition of "intervention" differs between time and space, such that where government participation in manufacturing activity will be considered an obstacle to private sector development in the USA; in China, such a move would be considered strategic. Similarly, the ban on slavery and child labour in today's developed countries, including the USA, which are not considered interventions now, were interpreted as "unnecessary interference" in the operations of the market, as they placed artificial entry barriers to the labour market as well as distortions on wages, with some efficiency impacts (Chang, 2002).

Hughes (2003) also argues that market failure imposes an artificial limit on what government can do—and, by implication, cannot do—when other goals (example equity, freedom, social cohesion, etc) may underpin state action.

An ideological criticism of market failure is that it is a tool used by the West to impose its vision of democracy and capitalism on developing nations through the so-called structural adjustment programs, with such devastating impacts as collapse of local industrialization, mass unemployment, poverty, and informationalization. In other words, market failure is can be used as a deliberate smoke screen by western governments or their supranational organizations to advance their neoliberal economic and political motives that ultimately serve to benefit them.

Technical criticisms, which deal with the purported causes of market failure and the effectiveness of state action, include the view that certain types of market failure (e.g., imperfect competition, imperfect information) are beneficial rather than harmful to the economy in the form encouraging dynamic efficiency and innovation. For instance, Karl Marx and latter Joseph Schumpeter observed that, in real world markets which are uncompetitive, old industries are progressively supplanted by new and better ones through research and invention, a process Schumpeter described as "creative destruction", which would be impossible under perfect competition and perfect information.

Another view is that government intervention can lead to "government failure"—the situation where society is made worse-off as a result of government attempt to correct market failure. In other words, government failure is the 'public' version of market failure, in which resources become less optimally allocated than if no intervention is made. Common examples of government failure include regulatory capture (or hijacking of a regulatory body by an industry or interest groups it is meant to regulate); rent-seeking (or influencing public policy through lobbying or other mechanism to by groups to inure to their benefit); and moral hazard tied to government subsidy.

Two practical criticisms of market failure, which relate to the problems of applying the theory, are as follows: first, it fails to specify the precise point at which state intervention is warranted (Hughes, 2003); second, that it fails to delineate the limits of state action (Walsh, 1995 cited in Hughes, 2003).

5. Evaluation

In giving a judgment on the relevance of market failure in explaining state action, it is vital first to note the variability in the debate over the usefulness of market failure. While it is literally possible to contest every aspect of the theory, three areas of dispute are noteworthy, which I shall briefly tackle below.

The first issue of contention is the primacy between the state and the market, that is to say, whether the state existed before the market or the market gave birth to the state. Market theorists claim that markets emerged spontaneously, universally and independent of the state, and rather trace the origins of the state to the first collective efforts to tackle market failure, specifically as a "market-type" contractual solution—that is, individuals voluntarily entering into contract to set up the state—to the collective action problem of providing the public good of law and order, particularly the security of private property, which is considered a necessary and sufficient pre-condition for markets to work (Chang, 2002). On the hand, economic historians and institutional economists insist that the state was the major architect in the development of the market, specifically by enacting property law, enforcing contracts, and making other arrangements necessary for the market to function.

The second kind of dispute in the discourse about the relevance of market failure relate to the view of the market, the economy, state and politics. For adherents of market failure, the ideal or most efficient system of resource allocation is through the market, which is theoretically defined as the perfect competitive market; and is a distinguishable sphere from the state, and functions properly with little or no state intervention. Moreover, the market is equated to the economy, whose performance is directly tied to that of the former. The state and politics, to neoliberal or pro-market failure theorists, are made up short-sighted and self-seeking individuals who cannot be trusted to provide benevolent moral guidance to society. On the other hand, institutional economists see the market as a politically-constructed institution that is inseparable from politics;

therefore, political action cannot be read as "interventions" in, or "distortions" to, the market, but as necessary to ensure its proper functioning. Also, they argue that human actions, including those of politicians and civil servants, are not always driven by pure self-interest; other motivations, including charity, nationalism, public service ethic, may underlie public action (Chang, 2003).

The third kind of dispute is over the causes of market failure and the means for correcting it. While some market economists insist that markets do not fail at all and therefore require no kind of intervention whatsoever, others believe they do, albeit differing over what kind of approach to use. While anti-interventionist market economists prefer "market-based solutions" to market failures, pro-interventionist market economists or institutions, including the IMF and World Bank, advocate state intervention to address market failure.

In presenting my personal opinion on the potency of market failure theory in explaining and justifying government action, I propose the following four questions for use as my criteria for assessment:

1. How realistic are the theory's assumptions about the market and the state?
2. How effective is it in explaining the origins and role of the state as well as differences in government action?
4. How consistent is the theory?
5. How effective can it be used as a practical guide for public policy?

Reasonability of Assumptions about the Market and the State
Market failure's view of the ideal market is highly abstract or utopian, making it unattainable. Also, its bleak assessment of the state is inaccurate, as not all state action amounts to inefficiency and waste. Third, by artificially diving society into market and public spheres, market failure overlooks the range of actors and networks that the market is intertwined with. Lastly, its antagonistic view of the market-state relationship ignores the many ways in which the two institutions can collaborate to achieve broader societal goals. For instance, developmentalists states such as Japan and South Korea provide a good example of how the state and the market can forge close collaboration to achieve national economic development aspirations. While pro-market economists argue that the prospects of these nations would be much higher if the private

sector was or is allowed to allocate resources independently, this can only be a guess, with no empirical proof. In Africa, on the other hand, where governments happily and rapidly embraced the 'Washington consensus' and shirked off the state's role in economic development following the late 1970 global recession to a private sector that was largely undeveloped, economic decline, poverty, inflation, and decades of struggle have been the outcomes of the structural adjustment programs introduced by the two Breton-Woods institutions: the World Bank and the IMF

Effectiveness in Explaining the Origins and Role of the State, including differences in State Action

Market failure's claim that the state arose because of market failure simply contradicts historical evidence (Chang, 2003), not least in Africa where traditional states existed in communitarian societies long before colonialism brought capitalism. Moreover, its explanation of the role of the state, as a provider of only those goods and services which it discovered the market was failing to provide, is inadequate in explaining how and why different states came to acquire the different functions they perform, as well as why they continue to provide different goods and services or own different assets in the countries in which they operate, including those having or claiming to promote a market system, such as the UK and the USA. For example, the theory says nothing about why postal service is sorely owned and provided by the US government, while in the UK it is owned and managed as a public-private partnership.

Consistency

The theory is laden with several contradictions. For example, it has faith in the state's ability to correct certain failures (e.g., public goods) but not others (e.g., imperfect information). The argument is used to justify the US government's subsidy to American farmers, yet oppose the same policy in Africa. Indeed, the same logic can be used to justify both laissez-faire and planned economies, legitimately. Market failure presents itself as an objective tool when it is in fact value-laden—to label certain market outcomes such as information asymmetry as 'failures' but not others such as inequality is political.

Applicability

Market failure is an inadequate manual of public policy. This is because not only does it fail to establish the exact point where intervention is needed (Hughes, 2003), but also it fails to offer any practical advice for developing the best remedy for curing any market failure. In addition, it gives no definitive scope of government action.

6. Alternative Ideas

The most popular alternative model for explaining public policy is the institutional political economy approach (IPE) advanced by institutional economists such as Ha-Joon Chang, which incorporates politics and institutions. At the heart of this approach is the notion that the state is a complex institution constituting of individuals, norms, values and other institutions, which are constantly interacting with, and affecting, one another. And because human behaviour is influenced and modified by the institutions they interact with, in this case "public institutions" that are fashioned on non-selfish values such as public service ethic, social reform and nationalism, then "public" or state action is not necessarily driven by selfish motivations, but by these greater ideals. IPE thus emphasizes an understanding of the broader institutional context in which public policy takes place (for a fuller explanation of the IPE approach to understanding the state, see Chang, 2002).

Another approach would be a historical analysis of the state—to know why and how the modern state came to acquire the functions it has. The final option is conducting a survey of government activities in a range of countries and ascertaining the reasons for any observed differences. These later two approaches can help factor in two factors fundamental to appreciating the differences in state action: history and context.

7. Conclusion

This paper has examined the notion of market failure, which is undoubtedly one of the most influential contemporary theories for justifying, explaining and supposedly guiding government role and action in society. The underlying principle and logic of the market failure doctrine is that governments exist only to correct the inherent failings of the market, which is attributed to its structural limitations, which include the following: the provision of public goods, the incidence of externality, the occurrence of monopoly, and the phenomenon of imperfect information. Four common prescribed solutions for tackling market failure are government provision, taxation, subsidy and regulation.

Having undertaken a thorough interrogation of market failure, this paper has identified a number of loopholes in the theory, ranging from its basic assumptions about the market, the state and human behaviour, to its practical application, all of which have been detailed above. It is therefore concluded that while market failure offers some helpful intuition on what *governments (can) do*, it fails to provide a compelling and thorough answer to the question *why governments exist?* Besides, the theory is blind to its western-centered roots. Alternative approaches, such as the emerging new institutional political economy approach propounded by leading institutional economists such as Ha-Joo Chang, which makes political factors and the role of institutions central to understanding the nature, behaviour and relationship between the market and the state, including those actions undertaken within and around the boundaries of the state. As well, historical analysis and empirical studies of different state compositions and functions can provide some inductive reasoning and insight into why governments exist and do what they do.

Reference

Chang, H. 2002. 'Breaking the Mould: An Institutionalist Political Economy Alternative to the Neo-Liberal Theory of the Market and the State. *Cambridge Journal of Economics*, 26, 539-559

Cobin, J.M. 2009. '*A Primer on Modern Themes in Free Market Economics and Policy* [online]. Florida, Universal-Publishers. Available from: http://books.google.ca/books?id=t13-RzOF-4kC&printsec=frontcover&dq=A+Primer+on+Modern+Themes+in+Free+Market+Economics+and+Policy:+Second+Edition&hl=en&sa=X&ei=5uVRUfi0L-eWiAKdwoCoBQ&ved=0CDIQ6AEwAA#v=onepage&q=A%20Primer%20on%20Modern%20Themes%20in%20Free%20Market%20Economics%20and%20Policy%3A%20Second%20Edition&f=false [Assessed March 20134]

Flynn, N. 2011. 'Public Policy and Management: Perspectives and Issues'. *Course Introduction and Overview*. 2ed. London: Centre for Financial and Management Studies, SOAS, University of London

Foldvary, F.E. 2006. 'The Market Never Fail' [online]. APE Conference. Las Vegas, April 4. Available from: http://foldvary.net/works/mnflv1.html [Accessed March 2013]

Hughes, O. 2003. 'The Role of Government'. In: O Hughes. 2003 *Public Management and Administration*. London: Mcmillan, 71-93

World Bank. 1997. 'The Evolving Role of the State'. In: World Bank, 1997 *World Development Report: The State in a Changing World*. World Bank, 19-28